Brush Well

A Look at Dental Care

by Katie Bagley

Consultant:
Lori Gagliardi, RDA, RDH
Former President
California Dental Hygienists' Association

Bridgestone Books
an imprint of Capstone Press
Mankato, Minnesota

Bridgestone Books are published by Capstone Press
151 Good Counsel Drive, P.O. Box 669, Mankato, Minnesota 56002
http://www.capstone-press.com

Library of Congress Cataloging-in-Publication Data
Bagley, Katie.
    Brush well: a look at dental care/by Katie Bagley.
    p. cm.—(Your health)
    Includes bibliographical references and index.
    ISBN 0-7368-0969-4
    1. Dental care—Juvenile literature. 2. Teeth—Care and hygiene—Juvenile literature.
3. Dentistry—Juvenile literature. [1. Teeth—Care and hygiene. 2. Dental care.] [DNLM:
1. Oral hygiene—Juvenile literature. WU 113.6 B146b 2002] I. Title. II. Your health (Mankato, Minn.)
RK63 .B34 2002
617.6'01—dc21   00-012533

Summary: An introduction to teeth, brushing, flossing, and the importance of good dental care.

Editorial Credits
Sarah Lynn Schuette, editor; Karen Risch, product planning editor; Linda Clavel, designer
    and illustrator; Jeff Anderson, photo researcher

Photo Credits
Capstone Press/Gary Sundermeyer, 8
EyeWire Images, 1
Gregg R. Andersen, cover, 4, 12, 14, 16, 18, 20
Kent Wood, 10
Visuals Unlimited/John D. Cunningham, 6

**Bridgestone Books thanks Mari Schuh, Connie Colwell, and Franklin Elementary School,
Mankato, Minnesota, for providing photo shoot locations.**

1 2 3 4 5 6 07 06 05 04 03 02

Table of Contents

Your Teeth Are Important

Your teeth help you chew, speak, and smile. Most kids have 20 primary teeth. Primary teeth fall out and permanent teeth grow in. Adults have 32 permanent teeth.

permanent teeth
adult teeth that
do not fall out

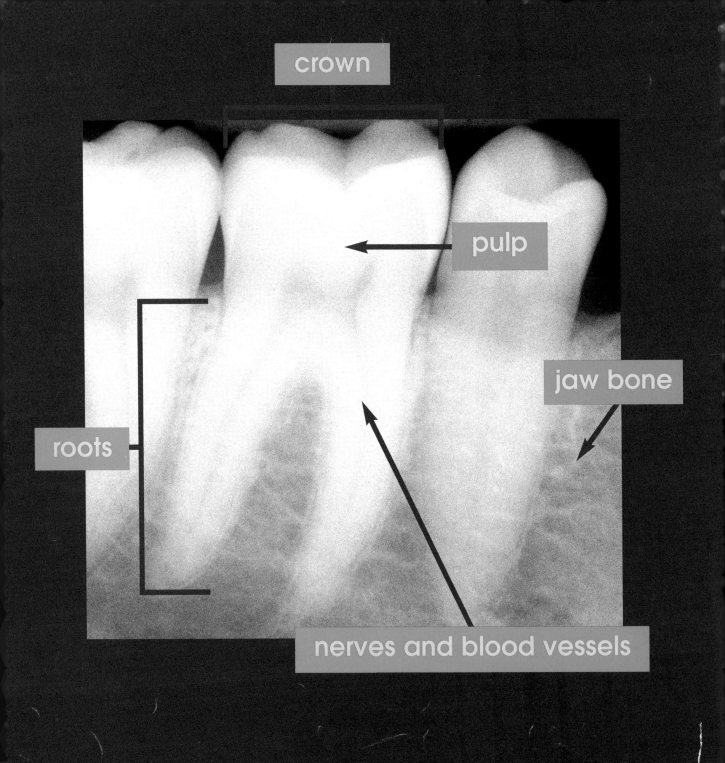

Your Teeth: Inside and Out

A tooth has many parts. The crown is the part you can see. Enamel covers the whole tooth. This hard, white substance protects your teeth. The soft pulp inside the tooth has nerves and blood vessels. Dentin is around the pulp. Roots are under the gums and jaw bone.

dentin

a hard substance that makes up the body of a tooth

Guess What?

The enamel on your teeth is the hardest part of your body.

Types of Teeth

Teeth are different sizes and shapes. Each type of tooth does a different job. Canines and incisors shred and tear food. These teeth help you bite food. Premolars and molars have flat tops to grind food. They help you chew food.

Guess What?

This tooth has a cavity.
Dentists put metal fillings
or clear fillings in cavities.

Cavities

A cavity is a decayed or broken down part of a tooth. Plaque (PLAK) builds up on tooth enamel and traps bits of food. The sugar in food mixes with bacteria in your mouth and forms acid. Acid breaks down tooth enamel. Acid causes cavities.

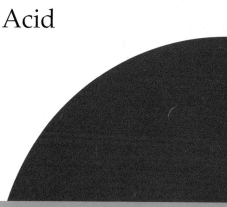

plaque
a coating made from food, bacteria, and saliva that forms on teeth

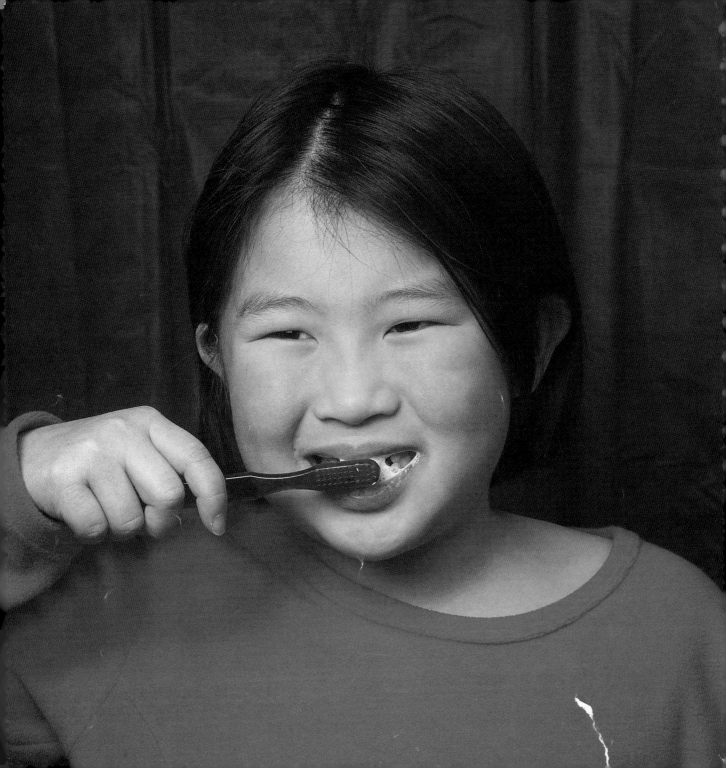

Brushing Well

Brushing your teeth helps remove food, plaque, and acid. You should brush your teeth and tongue after you eat and before you go to bed. Brushing well helps you have fresh breath and prevents cavities.

Toothbrushes and Toothpaste

Toothbrushes come in different sizes and shapes. Ask an adult to help you find the right size toothbrush. You should replace your toothbrush when it is worn out. Using toothpaste with fluoride is important. Fluoride helps make tooth enamel strong.

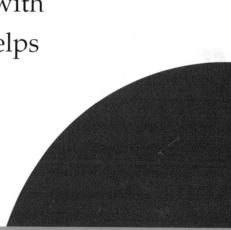

fluoride
a substance put onto teeth to make enamel stronger; fluoride is in most toothpaste.

Flossing Your Teeth

Dental floss removes food and plaque from between your teeth. Flossing keeps your gums healthy. You should floss once a day after you brush your teeth.

dental floss
a thin strand of thread used to clean between teeth

17

Try This!

Have yogurt or fresh fruit as a snack. These foods are good for your teeth.

Eating Right

Eating right helps your teeth stay healthy. Drinking milk and eating foods with calcium makes teeth strong. Cookies, candy, and soft drinks are bad for your teeth. Sugar in these foods causes plaque and acid to form. Eating less sugar helps prevent cavities.

calcium

a soft, white mineral found in teeth, bones, and some foods

Toothpaste was invented in the 1800s. Some people cleaned their teeth with charcoal or chalk before toothpaste was invented.

Dental Care

You should visit your dentist twice each year. Dental hygienists show you how to brush and floss correctly. They clean your teeth and check for cavities. Dentists fix cavities. Dentists also put sealants on teeth to prevent cavities.

sealant
a substance put onto teeth to prevent cavities

Hands On: Tooth Enamel

Acid forms in your mouth after you eat sugary foods. In this experiment you will see how a different type of acid breaks down a hard eggshell.

What You Need

Measuring cup
Bottle of vinegar
Empty peanut butter jar with lid
Egg

What You Do

1. Measure one cup of vinegar and pour it into the empty jar.
2. Place the egg in the jar and close the lid.
3. Let the jar sit overnight.
4. What happens to the egg?

The vinegar eats away at the eggshell. The eggshell disappears. The acid in your mouth breaks down tooth enamel in the same way. Brushing your teeth helps remove acid and prevents cavities.

Words to Know

acid (ASS-id)—a liquid that breaks down tooth enamel

bacteria (bak-TIHR-ee-uh)—small living cells found outside and inside of the body

cavity (KAV-uh-tee)—a decayed or broken down part of a tooth; brushing well helps prevent cavities.

crown (KROUN)—the top part of a tooth

enamel (e-NAM-uhl)—a hard, white coating found on teeth

gum (GUHM)—the firm, pink flesh around the base of a person's teeth

root (ROOT)—the part of a tooth that grows below the gum

Read More

Hodgkins, Fran. *Dental Hygienists.* Community Helpers. Mankato, Minn.: Bridgestone Books, 2001.

Silverstein, Alvin, Virginia Silverstein, and Laura Silverstein Nunn. *Tooth Decay and Cavities.* My Health. New York: Franklin Watts, 1999.

Internet Sites

BrainPop Movie: Teeth
http://www.brainpop.com/health/digestive/teeth/index.weml

Taking Care of Your Teeth
http://kidshealth.org/kid/stay_healthy/body/teeth.html

The Wisdom Tooth
http://www.umanitoba.ca/outreach/wisdomtooth/index.html

Index

5/02